AF480672

INNOVATIVE SOLUTIONS FOR SOCIAL CHANGE

THE ROLE OF SOCIAL PSYCHOLOGY FOR CRAFTING A BETTER WORLD

DR. MINAKSHI BANSAL

Contents

Contents

Prayer

"Om Bhadram Karnebhih Shrinuyama Devah
Bhadram Pashyemakshabhiryajatrah
Sthirairangais Tushtuvamsastanubhih
Vyashema Devahitam Yadayuh
Svasti Na Indro Vriddhashravah
Svasti Nah Pusha Vishwavedah
Svasti Nastarkshyo Arishtanemih
Svasti No Brihaspatir Dadhatu
Om Shantih Shantih Shantih"

This mantra is a prayer for universal well-being, invoking the blessings of various deities for protection, health, and happiness. It emphasizes the importance of experiencing the auspicious through all senses and living a life aligned with divine purpose. The repetition of "Shantih" at the end signifies a deep desire for peace in the individual, the environment, and the universe at large. This mantra is often recited as a prayer for peace, prosperity, and the physical and spiritual well-being of all beings.

ᗡᗡᗡ

About The Author

Dr. Minakshi Bansal, born in the bustling metropolis of Delhi, India, has led a life steeped in artistry, scholarly pursuit, and an unwavering commitment to societal betterment. Following her marriage, she relocated to Ahmedabad, Gujarat, where she has since blossomed into a multifaceted beacon of inspiration for many. Dr. Minakshi is not only recognized as a gifted artist in the realm of Fine Arts but also as an esteemed author, a devoted social worker and a dedicated research scholar in Psychology. Her journey, marked by a profound dedication to elevating those around her, especially the downtrodden and underprivileged children of society, is a testament to her deep-seated belief in the transformative power of engagement and empathy.

From her earliest days, Minakshi was distinguished by an insatiable appetite for reading. Her literary universe was inhabited by characters and narratives that spanned ethical tales, motivational and inspirational stories, and the mythic parables imbued with life lessons.

This voracious reading habit was not merely for personal edification but was driven by a desire to distill and disseminate the essence of these narratives to foster the development of students and peers alike. She was particularly captivated by the lives and teachings of historical figures and spiritual leaders such as Adi Shankaracharya, Swami Vivekananda, Dr. APJ Abdul Kalam, Mahamana Pandit Madan Mohan Malviya, Mahatma Gandhi, Sardar Vallabhai Patel, and Vinoba Bhave, among others. Their philosophies and life stories fueled her ambition to embody their ideals of resilience, selflessness, and relentless pursuit of knowledge.

Dr. Minakshi's academic and practical engagement with psychology has been equally noteworthy. As a research scholar, her focus has been on exploring the intricate tapestry of the human psyche, aiming to unlock the potential for psychological well-being and societal harmony. Her scholarly work is complemented by her active involvement in social work, where she employs her academic insights to make tangible differences in the lives of the underprivileged.

Her endeavours in social work are characterized by an innovative approach that combines traditional wisdom with contemporary psychological practices to address the multifaceted challenges faced by these communities.

Her artistic talents, another facet of her diverse capabilities, are not merely a personal passion but also serve as a medium through which she communicates and connects with others. Her art, rich in symbolism and emotional depth, reflects her philosophical inquiries and social concerns, offering viewers a glimpse into the breadth of her intellect and the depth of her compassion.

In addition to her contributions to the arts and social sciences, Dr. Minakshi has embraced the healing arts of Pranic Healing, mastering the techniques developed by Master Choa Kok Sui. This practice, which focuses on the manipulation of Prana or life energy to heal the body and aura, has been both a personal journey of discovery and a means through which she extends her healing touch to others.

Her proficiency in Pranic Healing is complemented by her advocacy and teaching of various forms of meditation aimed at rejuvenation, personal betterment, and the cultivation of harmony within individuals and communities alike.

Dr. Minakshi's life is a narrative of relentless pursuit, not just of personal achievement but of the upliftment and empowerment of society at large. Her diverse interests and talents—spanning the arts, literature, psychology, and the healing practices—converge on a singular path of service. She embodies the spirit of the luminaries who inspired her, channelling their legacy through her actions and teachings. Through her books, art, and social initiatives, she continues to inspire a new generation to embark on their own journeys of self-discovery, resilience, and altruism.

Her commitment to social betterment, particularly her focus on uplifting underprivileged children, reflects a deep understanding of the transformative potential of education and personal development. By integrating her knowledge of psychology, her artistic sensibilities, and her healing practices, Dr. Bansal has developed a holistic approach to social work that addresses both the immediate needs and the long-term well-being of the communities she serves.

As an author, Dr. Minakshi's writings offer a blend of inspirational insights, practical wisdom, and reflective contemplations drawn from her extensive reading and life experiences. Her books serve as a guide for those seeking to navigate the complexities of life with grace, resilience, and purpose. Through her narratives, she extends an invitation to her readers to explore the depths of their own potential and to contribute meaningfully to the collective well-being of society.

In Dr. Minakshi Bansal, we find a remarkable synthesis of the artist, the scholar, the healer, and the social activist. Her life's work stands as a beacon of hope and a source of inspiration for individuals seeking to make a difference in the world. Her story is a compelling reminder of the power of individual action, rooted in compassion and driven by a profound commitment to the betterment of humanity. Dr. Minakshi's legacy is not just in the tangible outcomes of her efforts but in the enduring spirit of inquiry, empathy, and service that she embodies.

Preface

As we face increasingly complex global challenges—from climate change and inequality to migration and cultural conflicts—the need for innovative solutions has never been more urgent. Social psychology offers us tools and insights that are essential for addressing these issues. By understanding the underlying psychological mechanisms that drive social behaviors, we can develop more effective interventions and programs that resonate deeply with individuals and communities alike.

The relevance of social psychology in driving social change is multifaceted. It not only helps us comprehend how people think and feel about various issues but also how they are likely to behave under different circumstances. This understanding is critical for designing policies and initiatives that can lead to real and lasting change. Throughout this book, we explore several key areas where social psychology can be applied, from enhancing community engagement and resolving conflicts to promoting health, environmental sustainability, and more.

Each chapter of this book is dedicated to unpacking a specific area where social psychology has been applied to effect change. We begin by exploring foundational concepts, such as how attitudes are formed and the influence of group dynamics on individual behavior. This sets the stage for deeper discussions on more targeted issues, such as the psychological underpinnings of prejudice and discrimination and how these can be effectively challenged and overcome.

The book also addresses the impact of modern technology on social behavior, a timely topic given the pervasive influence of digital media on our daily lives. We examine how virtual interactions can shape our perceptions of reality and influence everything from our self-esteem to our political opinions. Additionally, we consider the psychological aspects of environmental behavior, discussing how people can be motivated to adopt more sustainable practices in their personal and professional lives.

In later chapters, we turn our attention to the role of leadership in social movements, the emotional aspects of social participation, and the ways in which volunteering and civic engagement are influenced by psychological factors. Each of these areas provides unique insights into how social change can be initiated and sustained over time.

One of the core themes of this book is the idea that effective social change requires a comprehensive approach that considers not only the economic and political dimensions of issues but also their psychological aspects. This holistic view can empower activists, policymakers, and everyday citizens to create strategies that are not only effective in the short term but also enduring.

We also discuss the future of social psychology in social change efforts, identifying emerging trends and challenges that will shape the field in the years to come. This forward-looking perspective is crucial for preparing current and future generations to continue the work of crafting a better world.

This book is intended for a broad audience, including students and professionals in psychology, sociology, and related fields, as well as activists, policymakers, and anyone interested in the intersection of psychology and social change. By providing a comprehensive overview of how psychological insights can be applied to solve real-world problems, we aim to inspire readers to think creatively and critically about their own roles in promoting social change.

As we conclude this preface, it is my hope that this book will serve as both a guide and an inspiration for those looking to make a difference in the world. The journey toward social change is often complex and challenging, but with the insights provided by social psychology, we have the tools necessary to navigate this terrain more effectively. Let us move forward with the knowledge that our actions, informed by a deep understanding of the social fabric of humanity, can lead to significant and positive transformations in our communities and beyond.

ONE

Introduction to Social Psychology and Social Change

Social psychology offers a lens through which we can understand and address the myriad challenges faced by societies. It delves into how individual thoughts, feelings, and behaviors are influenced by the actual, imagined, or implied presence of others. This understanding is crucial when considering how social change can be initiated and sustained. At its core, social psychology examines the powerful role of environmental and cognitive factors in shaping our interactions and behaviors, making it an essential field for anyone interested in fostering social change.

The relevance of social psychology to social change is evident when we consider the broad range of human interactions and the profound influence these interactions have on societal norms and policies. Social psychologists study attitudes, social perceptions, cultural influences, group behaviors, and other social factors that contribute significantly to societal dynamics. By understanding these elements, we can develop strategies that promote positive social change, aiming for outcomes that enhance societal well-being and promote more equitable communities.

Social psychologists use various theories to explain how and why people behave the way they do within a society. One key theory is the theory of planned behavior, which suggests that behavior is driven not only by personal attitudes but also by social norms and perceived control over the behavior. This theory can be applied to social change initiatives by helping to predict how changes in attitudes and perceptions might lead to desired behavioral outcomes. For example, if we aim to increase recycling within a community, understanding the community's attitudes towards recycling, their awareness of environmental norms, and their perceived difficulties in recycling can guide more effective community planning and policy-making.

Another fundamental aspect of social psychology relevant to social change is the concept of social influence, which includes conformity, compliance, and obedience. These phenomena show how group dynamics can affect individual behavior, sometimes leading to significant changes in social norms and behaviors. Movements for social change often rely on these principles to gather support and promote action. For instance, influential leaders or groups can inspire others to adopt new behaviors or support social causes by effectively leveraging their influence.

Social identity theory also plays a critical role in understanding social change. This theory explores how individuals' self-concepts are derived from perceived membership in social groups. It explains phenomena such as in-group favoritism, which can lead to prejudice and discrimination. Recognizing these patterns is essential for developing interventions that promote more inclusive societies. Programs that foster intergroup dialogue and understanding can mitigate the negative effects of in-group bias, helping to create communities that value diversity and equality.

Moreover, social psychologists have explored how emotions influence collective movements. Emotions can be a driving force behind the mobilization of social movements. For example, collective anger and injustice have historically been powerful motivators for political and social action. Understanding the emotional underpinnings of social movements can help organizers better craft their messages to resonate emotionally with a broader audience, thereby garnering greater support and facilitating more profound social change.

In terms of application, social psychology has practical implications for designing policies and interventions that effectively address social issues. By applying insights from social psychology, policymakers can craft initiatives that consider human behavior's complexities, thereby enhancing the effectiveness of these initiatives. For instance, when trying to reduce urban violence, interventions that consider social identity, group norms, and individual behaviors—as informed by social psychological research—may be more effective than those that do not.

Ultimately, the integration of social psychology into social change efforts offers a powerful tool for addressing complex social issues. By understanding the intricate dynamics of human behavior in social contexts, we can better design interventions that are not only effective but also sustainable. As we continue to face global challenges, from inequality to climate change, the insights provided by social psychology will be invaluable in crafting innovative solutions that are informed by a deep understanding of the social forces at play.

ᐅᐅᐅ

"Understanding the intricate tapestry of human behavior is the first step towards influencing societal norms and enacting lasting change. Through social psychology, we uncover the motivations behind actions, guiding us toward more effective interventions. Let this knowledge empower us to craft solutions that resonate deeply within communities."

▷▷▷

TWO
UNDERSTANDING HUMAN BEHAVIOR

Understanding human behavior is pivotal in deciphering the psychological factors that guide our actions and decisions. Human behavior is influenced by a complex interplay of cognitive processes, environmental variables, and past experiences. By exploring these psychological factors, we can gain insights into how individuals make decisions and how these decisions can be influenced or changed, which is particularly relevant in the context of promoting positive social change.

Cognitive Biases and Decision Making

At the heart of human behavior lies decision-making, often guided by various cognitive biases. These biases are systematic patterns of deviation from norm or rationality in judgment, where the influences of mental

constructs can skew our decisions. For example, the confirmation bias leads people to favor information that confirms their preconceptions, irrespective of whether the information is true. This bias can significantly impact social behavior, such as in the formation of polarized groups in society, where each group selectively accumulates evidence to support their views, disregarding contradicting evidence. Understanding these biases helps in designing interventions that can promote more informed decision-making in community and organizational settings.

The Role of Emotions in Behavior

Emotions profoundly influence human behavior. They can dictate our responses to various situations, from our interaction with others to our performance in tasks. For instance, fear can either prompt us to flee from danger or paralyze us, inhibiting any response. In the context of social change, emotions can drive or hinder participation in movements. Anger and outrage may mobilize populations against perceived injustices, while fear and despair might discourage involvement. By acknowledging the emotional drivers behind behavior, change agents can better strategize their approaches, ensuring they elicit the desired emotional responses that align with their goals of promoting change.

Social and Environmental Influences

Human behavior is also greatly shaped by the social and physical environment. From a young age, the norms and values imparted by our culture influence our behavior patterns. Social influences include family, friends, education, and media—all of which play pivotal roles in shaping attitudes and behaviors. Environmental factors like living conditions, economic stability, and community structures also impact behavior. Understanding these influences is crucial for creating effective social interventions that encourage sustainable behaviors. For instance, community-based programs that leverage strong local ties and address specific local needs are often more successful in changing behaviors sustainably.

Psychological Theories of Behavior Change

Several psychological theories have been developed to explain and predict changes in behavior, which are crucial for designing interventions that effectively address social problems. The Theory of Planned Behavior, for example, posits that behavior is directly influenced by an individual's intention to perform the behavior, which is itself influenced by attitudes toward the behavior, subjective norms, and perceived behavioral control. This theory can be utilized to shape interventions by identifying and altering these factors to nudge individuals towards desired behaviors.

Another influential theory, the Transtheoretical Model of Behavioral Change, suggests that people go through five stages when changing behavior: precontemplation, contemplation, preparation, action, and maintenance. Interventions that cater to the specific needs of individuals at each stage are more likely to be successful. For instance, those in the precontemplation stage may benefit from awareness-raising campaigns, while those in the preparation stage might need tools and resources to facilitate change.

Motivation and Human Behavior

Motivation is another key driver of human behavior that merits attention. It encompasses the processes that govern our enthusiasm and persistence to pursue particular actions. Motivation can be intrinsic, originating within the individual because the behavior itself is rewarding, or extrinsic, driven by external rewards. Understanding what motivates people can help in designing better policies and interventions. For example, in educational settings, recognizing that intrinsic motivation often leads to better learning outcomes can lead to pedagogical strategies that focus on making learning enjoyable and meaningful rather than solely on external rewards like grades.

Understanding the psychological factors that influence human actions and decisions provides a foundation for developing more effective strategies for social change. By exploring cognitive biases, the role of emotions, social and environmental influences, psychological theories of behavior change, and motivational drives, we can devise comprehensive approaches that address the root causes of behaviors. This not only helps in mitigating adverse behaviors but also in promoting positive actions, ultimately fostering a more just and sustainable society.

❦❦❦

"True leadership in social movements involves more than just guiding others; it demands vision, integrity, and a profound empathy for the human condition. Effective leaders don't just create followers, they nurture new leaders, spreading the flames of activism. Their impact is measured not just in immediate outcomes, but in the sustained momentum of the movement."

ᗅᗅᗅ

THREE

THE POWER OF ATTITUDES

Attitudes are central to understanding and influencing human behavior, particularly in the context of social transformation. An attitude is a psychological tendency that is expressed by evaluating a particular entity with some degree of favor or disfavor. These evaluations, whether positive or negative, shape how individuals think, feel, and behave towards social issues, people, objects, and events. Understanding the formation of attitudes and how they can be modified is crucial for any effort aimed at achieving meaningful social change.

Formation of Attitudes

The formation of attitudes occurs through various channels, including direct experience, the influence of friends and family, and exposure to media. From early childhood, individuals are exposed to a wide range of attitudes in the environment around them, which they may adopt over time. For example, a child raised in a household that values education will likely develop a positive attitude toward school and learning. This process of attitude formation is also heavily influenced by social norms and cultural contexts, which provide a framework within which certain attitudes are seen as

"

acceptable or desirable.

Social learning theory highlights the role of observation and imitation in acquiring attitudes. People, especially children, learn attitudes by observing the behaviors of others and the consequences of these behaviors. If a behavior is rewarded, an observer may adopt the attitudes and behaviors consistent with that action. Moreover, cognitive dissonance theory suggests that people have a fundamental need to ensure that their beliefs, attitudes, and behaviors are consistent. When inconsistencies occur, such as behaving in a way that is opposite to one's attitude, individuals will feel discomfort and are motivated to change either their behavior or attitude to reduce this dissonance.

The Role of Communication in Shaping Attitudes

Communication plays a pivotal role in attitude formation and change. Through persuasive communication, such as public speeches, advertisements, or social media content, attitudes can be shaped and reshaped. The effectiveness of persuasive messages in changing attitudes is influenced by several factors, including the credibility of the source, the emotional appeal of the message, and the relevance of the message to the individual's personal circumstances. A credible source, one that is perceived as knowledgeable and trustworthy, is more likely to influence attitudes than a source with low credibility.

The elaboration likelihood model (ELM) of persuasion explains how attitudes change based on the depth of information processing involved. This model posits two routes to persuasion: the central and peripheral routes. The central route involves careful and thoughtful consideration of the true merits of the information presented, leading to more durable attitude change. In contrast, the peripheral route involves less scrutiny of the message and more reliance on peripheral cues such as the attractiveness or celebrity status of the messenger, leading to more temporary attitude changes. Effective social campaigns often need to address both routes to cater to different audiences and to ensure both immediate and long-lasting attitude changes.

Attitudes and Social Change

Changing attitudes is often a necessary step in social transformation. For instance, attitudes towards smoking have changed dramatically over the past few decades due to targeted public health campaigns that have altered public perceptions of smoking's social acceptability and health implications. Similarly, attitudes toward issues like recycling, drug use, and gender equality have evolved through concerted efforts that combine education, policy changes, and mass media campaigns.

For social change to occur, it is not enough for people to merely change their private attitudes. These new attitudes need to be translated into public norms and behaviors. This requires not only individual change but also collective action and reinforcement. Social movements, therefore, play a crucial role in mobilizing individuals to act on their attitudes and advocate for broader societal changes. The civil rights movement in the United States, for example, was not just about changing individual attitudes toward race but also about transforming these new attitudes into laws and societal norms.

To effectively foster social transformation through attitude change, interventions must be multifaceted. They should include strategies to inform and educate, to involve key influencers, and to provide social support for new behaviors. Additionally, recognizing the resistance to change that often accompanies deeply held attitudes is crucial. Strategies to overcome this resistance include providing clear, consistent, and credible information, creating opportunities for interpersonal communication, and ensuring that individuals feel competent to change their behaviors in line with their new attitudes.

Attitudes are powerful drivers of both individual behavior and social norms. By understanding how attitudes are formed and changed, social change agents can more effectively design interventions that not only shift individual perspectives but also foster broader societal transformation. The challenge lies not only in changing what people believe but also in ensuring that these new beliefs are reflected in their actions and societal structures, ultimately leading to sustainable change.

❧❧❧

"Volunteerism acts as the heartbeat of community engagement, pulsing with the altruistic desires of individuals seeking to make a difference. Each act of service weaves a stronger fabric of community resilience and social solidarity. As we give freely of ourselves, we receive much more in return—strengthening not just our communities, but our own sense of purpose and connection."

▷▷▷

FOUR

Social Influence and Group Dynamics

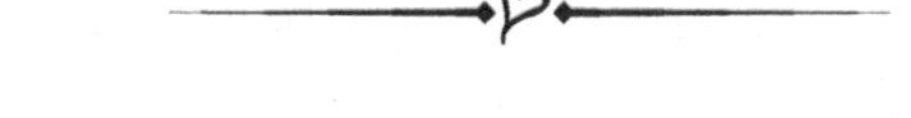

Social influence and group dynamics are integral aspects of understanding how individual behavior and societal norms are shaped. These elements reveal how interactions within a group can significantly affect an individual's actions, beliefs, and attitudes, often leading to conformity to group norms or changes in social behavior. This understanding is crucial for any effort to foster social change, as it helps identify ways to leverage group influence to promote positive behaviors and societal norms.

The Power of Social Influence

Social influence occurs when an individual's emotions, opinions, or behaviors are affected by others. This influence can take many forms, including conformity, compliance, and obedience, each playing a pivotal role in shaping societal norms. Conformity refers to the process of aligning one's beliefs, attitudes, and behaviors to those of a group. It is driven by the implicit or explicit pressure from others to fit in or to adhere to a perceived norm. For instance, in a social experiment where individuals are asked to match line lengths, the presence of others giving incorrect answers can lead someone to conform to the group's wrong answers, even if they initially know the correct response.

Compliance involves changing one's behavior at the request or direction of another person, often without internal agreement. This type of social influence is commonly leveraged in marketing and advertising, where calls to action ("Call now!", "Subscribe!") encourage people to behave in certain ways, even if they might not fully believe in the product or service. Obedience, on the other hand, involves a change of behavior to adhere to the commands of an authority figure. Historical experiments by Stanley Milgram demonstrated how far individuals are willing to go in obeying an authority, highlighting the powerful effects of authoritative influence on behavior.

Group Dynamics and Behavior

Group dynamics also play a crucial role in how social influence unfolds. The characteristics of a group, including its size, cohesiveness, structure, and the roles of its members, significantly affect how individuals think and act within it. For instance, smaller groups tend to have stronger cohesiveness, which can enhance conformity pressures. The presence of a cohesive group can significantly influence an individual's likelihood of adopting new behaviors or beliefs that are endorsed by the group.

The impact of group norms is another critical aspect of group dynamics. Norms are the shared expectations and rules that guide behavior within a group. They determine what is considered acceptable or unacceptable behavior within the group context. Once established, these norms can strongly influence individual behavior and can either be a force for positive change or reinforce negative behaviors. For instance, in a corporate setting, if the norm is to cut corners to achieve targets, new employees are likely to adopt this behavior to fit in, even if it goes against their personal or ethical standards.

Leveraging Group Dynamics for Social Change

Understanding the mechanics of group dynamics offers valuable insights for designing effective social change initiatives. For social movements or interventions to be successful, they often need to tap into existing group norms or create new norms that promote desired behaviors. This can be achieved through various strategies, such as engaging with influential group leaders, using public commitments, or fostering environments that encourage desired behaviors.

For example, public commitments can be a powerful tool in effecting change. When individuals publicly commit to a behavior, they are more likely to follow through to avoid dissonance between their public actions and their self-image. Social change campaigns can leverage this by encouraging people to make public pledges to perform environmentally friendly behaviors, like recycling or reducing energy use, thus setting new group norms.

Challenges and Considerations

While the potential of social influence and group dynamics in fostering change is considerable, there are challenges and ethical considerations to be mindful of. One of the primary concerns is the potential for groupthink, a psychological phenomenon where the desire for group harmony or conformity results in an irrational or dysfunctional decision-making outcome. It is crucial for groups to encourage open dialogue and critical thinking to avoid such pitfalls.

Moreover, efforts to change group norms or leverage social influence should always consider the ethical implications of influencing behavior. It is important to ensure that such interventions respect individual autonomy and promote genuinely beneficial social outcomes.

Social influence and group dynamics are powerful forces that can significantly impact individual behavior and societal norms. By understanding how these processes work, change agents can more effectively utilize these dynamics to foster positive social changes. Effective strategies will consider the nature of the group, the types of social influence at play, and the broader societal context to ensure that interventions are both successful and ethical. Ultimately, leveraging these insights in a thoughtful and strategic way can lead to profound and sustainable societal transformation.

ᗡᗡᗡ

"In the digital age, the internet shapes not just how we communicate, but how we think and act in our offline worlds. As our virtual connections grow, so too does the influence of every tweet, post, and share. We must navigate this new terrain wisely, harnessing its power to foster unity rather than division."

ᐅᐅᐅ

FIVE

Prejudice and Discrimination

Prejudice and discrimination are pervasive issues that significantly impact society, influencing everything from individual interactions to systemic policies. Understanding the roots of these behaviors is essential to developing effective strategies to combat discrimination and foster a more equitable society.

The Roots of Prejudice

Prejudice refers to preconceived opinions or attitudes about an individual or group that are not based on reason or actual experience. These biases often stem from a complex mix of psychological, social, and cultural factors. At the psychological level, prejudices can arise from the natural human tendency to categorize the world. This cognitive process simplifies social perception but can also lead to stereotyping, where people attribute specific characteristics to all members of a group, regardless of their individual differences.

Social identity theory helps explain the social roots of prejudice. This theory posits that individuals derive part of their identity from the social groups to which they belong, and they tend to favor their own groups (in-groups) while discriminating against others (out-groups). This favoritism can reinforce self-esteem but also leads to negative attitudes and behaviors toward those outside the in-group. Cultural influences also play a significant role, as societal norms and values shape attitudes toward different groups. Cultural narratives and media representations can perpetuate stereotypes, further embedding prejudices in the social fabric.

Discrimination and Its Impacts

Discrimination is the behavior that results from prejudiced attitudes. This can include actions such as exclusion, avoidance, and violence against individuals based on their group membership, such as race, gender, age, or sexual orientation. The impacts of discrimination are profound, affecting the psychological, economic, and physical well-being of those targeted. Discrimination not only harms individuals but also undermines social cohesion and economic productivity by marginalizing entire groups of people.

Strategies to Combat Discrimination

Addressing prejudice and discrimination requires a multi-faceted approach, encompassing education, policy interventions, and individual actions.

Education and Awareness

Education is a powerful tool in combating prejudice. By exposing individuals to different cultures, histories, and perspectives, educational programs can challenge existing stereotypes and reduce biased attitudes. Schools and universities play a crucial role in this regard by integrating multicultural education into their curricula and fostering an inclusive environment. Beyond formal education, media and public campaigns can also raise awareness about the harms of discrimination and the value of diversity.

Policy Interventions

Legislative and institutional policies are critical in addressing systemic discrimination. Anti-discrimination laws, such as those enforcing equal employment opportunities and fair housing, help protect individuals from discriminatory practices. However, policies need to be effectively enforced and accompanied by mechanisms for individuals to report discrimination and seek redress. Workplaces and organizations can also implement policies that promote diversity and inclusion, such as bias training programs, affirmative action plans, and transparent hiring practices.

Promoting Inclusivity and Dialogue

Creating inclusive spaces that promote dialogue between diverse groups can help reduce prejudices. Community programs that bring people together for shared activities can facilitate understanding and empathy. Initiatives like intergroup dialogues and community-building activities encourage direct interaction, which can challenge preconceived notions and reduce animosity between groups.

Individual Actions

Individuals can also play a role in combating prejudice by reflecting on their own biases and engaging in conversations about discrimination. Being an active bystander, calling out discriminatory behavior when it occurs, and supporting marginalized groups through advocacy and solidarity are ways individuals can contribute to societal change.

Prejudice and discrimination are deeply entrenched issues that require concerted efforts across various levels of society. By understanding the underlying causes and implementing comprehensive strategies to address these issues, we can move toward a more equitable and just society. Education, policy interventions, inclusive practices, and individual responsibility are all crucial in this endeavor. The journey toward reducing prejudice and discrimination is ongoing, and it requires persistent commitment and collaboration from all sectors of society to achieve lasting change.

ᗞᗞᗞ

"The echo chambers of social media amplify our biases but also offer a platform for diverse voices to be heard. To break through these walls, we must be willing to engage with opposing views, challenging our perspectives and encouraging growth. It is through this digital dialogue that society can evolve and embrace a broader worldview."

❥❥❥

6. Cultural Influences on Behavior

Culture profoundly influences human behavior and attitudes, serving as the backdrop against which social norms and practices are set. It encompasses the shared values, beliefs, norms, and practices of a group of people, and it guides how they interpret and interact with the world. The role of culture in shaping behaviors and attitudes towards social issues is pivotal, as it influences everything from policy decisions to individual actions within a society.

Understanding Cultural Influence

Culture provides the lens through which individuals see and understand the world, influencing their behaviors and attitudes. These cultural frameworks are not static but evolve over time, influenced by various factors such as economic changes, technological advancements, and interactions with other cultures. Despite these changes, certain core cultural values remain deeply ingrained within societies and continue to influence generations.

For instance, individualism and collectivism are cultural traits that significantly impact social behaviors and attitudes. Individualistic cultures, such as the United States and Western Europe, emphasize personal achievement and independence, affecting behaviors around self-expression, personal responsibility, and privacy. Conversely, collectivist cultures, found in many Asian and African countries, stress community and familial ties, influencing attitudes towards authority, conformity, and group welfare.

Culture and Social Norms

Cultural norms dictate what is considered acceptable or taboo within a society, influencing legal systems, education, business practices, and everyday social interactions. These norms are often so ingrained that individuals may not be consciously aware of them, yet they dictate actions in significant ways. For example, norms surrounding gender roles can deeply influence educational and career opportunities for men and women. In many cultures, traditional beliefs about gender roles may restrict women's participation in the workforce or in higher education, while men may face pressures to conform to expectations of stoicism and financial responsibility.

Cultural norms also shape responses to social issues such as mental health, immigration, and inequality. Attitudes towards mental health, for instance, vary widely across cultures. In some cultures, mental health issues are highly stigmatized, leading to underreporting and under-treatment of such conditions. In others, there is growing recognition and acceptance of mental health as a crucial component of overall health, leading to better support systems and resources.

Cultural Influence on Communication and Interaction

Culture influences not only what we communicate but how we communicate. Communication styles vary significantly from one culture to another and affect how people negotiate, how they express disagreement, and how they build relationships. High-context cultures, such as Japan and Arab countries, rely heavily on nonverbal cues and the context of the communication, where trust and relationships play a critical role in communications. In contrast, low-context cultures, such as the United States and Germany, emphasize direct and explicit communication.

These differences in communication styles can lead to misunderstandings and conflicts when individuals from different cultural backgrounds interact. Awareness and understanding of these differences are crucial in international relations, business, and multicultural societies, where effective communication is key to cooperation and harmony.

Cultural Adaptation and Social Change

As societies become more interconnected through globalization, cultural adaptation becomes increasingly important. Exposure to diverse cultures can lead to a blending of traditions and ideas, influencing social norms and behaviors across the globe. This blending can also spark social change by challenging traditional norms and introducing new perspectives on issues such as human rights, democracy, and environmental responsibility.

However, cultural adaptation also raises questions about the preservation of cultural identity and the potential for cultural imperialism, where dominant cultures overshadow or replace local cultures. Balancing respect for cultural diversity with the promotion of universal human rights is a significant challenge in the globalized world.

Culture plays a critical role in shaping behaviors and attitudes towards social issues. It influences how individuals perceive and interact with the world, dictates social norms, and affects communication styles. Understanding the impact of culture is essential for addressing social issues effectively, as it allows for more nuanced approaches that respect cultural differences while promoting positive change. As the world becomes increasingly globalized, the interplay between culture and social issues will continue to evolve, necessitating continuous adaptation and dialogue to foster a more inclusive and harmonious global society.

ﬤﬤﬤ

"Every individual has the capacity to influence their environment, but first, they must believe in that ability. Promoting self-efficacy within communities ignites a powerful catalyst for change—empowering individuals to act not out of obligation, but out of belief in their own impact. When people feel capable, they can achieve the extraordinary."

ᛏᛏᛏ

SEVEN

Communication for Change

Effective communication is fundamental to initiating and sustaining social change. It not only disseminates information but also builds understanding, fosters empathy, and encourages cooperation among diverse groups. Mastering effective communication techniques is therefore essential for anyone looking to influence social issues positively.

The Essence of Strategic Communication

Strategic communication involves the deliberate design and dissemination of messages to achieve specific social, political, or commercial goals. This form of communication is critical in change efforts as it helps align the message with the audience's values and needs, ensuring that it resonates and motivates action. The strategic communication process involves several key components: understanding the audience, crafting clear and compelling messages, choosing the appropriate channels for message dissemination, and evaluating the impact of those messages.

Understanding the Audience

The first step in effective communication is understanding who the audience is and what they value. This involves demographic research, but more importantly, psychographic and ethnographic research to grasp the audience's attitudes, beliefs, and behaviors. For social change communications, it's also crucial to understand the barriers and facilitators to change within the target community. This understanding can guide the tone, content, and delivery of messages to make them more impactful.

Crafting Messages

Once the audience is understood, the next step is crafting messages that resonate on an emotional and rational level. Messages need to be clear, concise, and relevant to the audience's interests and needs. They should ideally evoke an emotional response and provide a clear call to action. For social change, messages often need to counter prevailing narratives and offer a compelling alternative vision for the future. Storytelling can be particularly effective here, as narratives are more memorable than abstract data and can illustrate complex issues through relatable scenarios.

Choosing the Right Channels

The channels through which messages are communicated are as important as the messages themselves. Different channels have different reaches, credibility, and effects on the audience. Traditional media, social media, community meetings, and personal interactions can all be part of an integrated communication strategy. The choice of channel depends on the audience's media consumption habits and the resources available for the communication campaign. In today's digital age, social media platforms provide powerful tools for reaching large audiences quickly, although traditional media can still be crucial for reaching less connected populations.

Techniques for Effective Communication

Several techniques can enhance the effectiveness of communication, especially when the goal is to promote understanding and cooperation.

Active Listening

Active listening involves fully concentrating on what is being said rather than just passively hearing the message. This technique helps in building trust and understanding, as it shows the speaker that their views are valued. In contexts of social change, active listening can help mediators and change agents understand the concerns and motivations of different stakeholders, enabling them to address these issues more effectively in their communications.

Empathetic Communication

Empathy in communication involves understanding and sharing the feelings of another person. This can bridge divides and foster cooperation, especially in charged or divisive settings. Communicating with empathy involves acknowledging the other person's feelings and perspectives without judgment, which can help de-escalate conflicts and open up more collaborative dialogues.

Feedback Loops

Effective communication is not a one-way street. Establishing feedback loops allows communicators to understand how their messages are being received and to adjust strategies accordingly. This is particularly important in dynamic social environments where public opinion and social conditions can change rapidly. Feedback mechanisms can include surveys, comments on social media posts, community forums, and other interactive formats.

Visualization

Complex information can often be more easily understood and remembered when presented visually. Infographics, charts, videos, and other visual aids can help illustrate relationships and patterns that are difficult to communicate through text alone. For social change communications, visual storytelling can be particularly impactful, making abstract or large-scale problems more concrete and relatable.

Effective communication is a critical tool for promoting understanding and cooperation in efforts toward social change. By strategically designing and delivering messages, and by employing techniques such as active listening, empathetic communication, effective use of feedback, and visualization, change agents can more effectively engage and mobilize diverse audiences. These efforts not only spread information but also build the mutual understanding and collective will necessary to address complex social challenges.

ppp

"Environmental psychology teaches us that our surroundings influence our behavior in profound ways. By creating spaces that promote sustainability and community, we can naturally encourage behaviors that benefit all. Our environments are not just settings, but active participants in our daily lives and habits."

༄༄༄

EIGHT

PERSUASION TECHNIQUES

Persuasion is a critical element in promoting social change, as it involves not only influencing people's attitudes and beliefs but also motivating them to take action. Effective persuasion techniques are essential for advocates, leaders, and organizations aiming to garner support and mobilize individuals towards achieving a common goal. These techniques can range from the use of logical arguments to emotional appeals and are often most effective when they are thoughtfully and ethically applied.

Understanding the Principles of Persuasion

The effectiveness of persuasion rests on several psychological principles that can drive people to change their attitudes and behaviors. One of the most influential frameworks for understanding these principles is Robert Cialdini's theory of persuasion, which outlines six key principles: reciprocity, scarcity, authority, consistency, liking, and social proof.

Reciprocity

Reciprocity is the obligation to give when you receive. In the context of social change, this might mean that when an organization helps individuals or communities, those beneficiaries may be more inclined to support or advocate for the organization's goals in return. For example, a nonprofit that provides free educational resources may find that recipients are more willing to volunteer their time or donate to the cause.

Scarcity

Scarcity refers to the value that people attribute to things that are less available. Persuaders can frame their messages to highlight the uniqueness or the limited availability of an opportunity to engage in a social change effort. This can be seen in campaigns that emphasize a limited-time opportunity to join a cause or support a movement, thus creating a sense of urgency.

Authority

People tend to follow the lead of credible, knowledgeable experts. Effective social change campaigns often use spokespersons who have credibility and authority in the subject matter. This could include respected figures in a community or experts in a specific field whose endorsements or arguments can lend significant weight to the cause.

Consistency

People like to be consistent with the things they have previously said or done. Persuasion can involve encouraging individuals to make small commitments that align with the larger change being advocated. Once these smaller commitments are made, individuals are more likely to agree to larger requests that are in line with their initial commitments.

Liking

People are more easily persuaded by others that they like. Campaigns for social change can benefit from having relatable and charismatic leaders or representatives who are able to form strong emotional connections with the audience. Similarly, tailoring messages in a way that resonates with the values and experiences of the target audience can increase likability and effectiveness.

Social Proof

People will do things that they see other people are doing. In persuasion, showing that others are supporting a cause can encourage more people to do the same. This is why many campaigns use testimonials and stories of those who have already joined the movement, as a way to offer proof that participation is widespread and valued.

Advanced Persuasive Techniques

Beyond these principles, there are advanced techniques that can enhance the persuasiveness of a campaign:

Storytelling

Storytelling is a powerful persuasive tool because it allows individuals to see practical examples of how their involvement in a cause can lead to real change. Stories can convey emotions and personal experiences that statistics or abstract arguments cannot. Effective storytelling involves characters that the audience can empathize with, a narrative that engages and a resolution that inspires action.

Framing

Framing involves presenting an issue in a way that emphasizes certain aspects over others. How an issue is framed can greatly influence people's perceptions and reactions. For social change, positive framing (focusing on the benefits of participation) and negative framing (highlighting the consequences of inaction) can be used strategically to motivate different segments of the audience.

Emotional Appeals

While rational arguments are important, emotional appeals can directly impact an audience's subconscious motivators. Appeals to emotions such as fear, hope, anger, or happiness can be powerful, but they must be used ethically and carefully, as they carry the risk of manipulation if not handled with sensitivity to the audience's needs and contexts.

Persuasion is an art that requires understanding the audience, using principles of influence effectively, and applying advanced techniques such as storytelling, framing, and emotional appeals. By employing these methods thoughtfully and ethically, individuals and organizations can significantly enhance their ability to engage others and drive meaningful social change. Effective persuasion not only changes minds but also hearts, leading to greater participation and commitment to transformative actions.

ᐯᐯᐯ

"The resilience of a community in the face of
adversity is largely dependent on its social capital.
Trust, networks, and mutual support are not just
social niceties but lifelines during crises. Building
these bonds is essential for any community's ability
to survive, adapt, and thrive."

ᗡᗡᗡ

NINE

LEADERSHIP IN SOCIAL MOVEMENTS

Leadership plays a pivotal role in the success of social movements. Effective leaders are able to inspire action, guide new initiatives, and maintain momentum in long-term efforts to bring about change. The characteristics of these leaders, along with their strategies and behaviors, deeply influence the trajectory and outcomes of social movements.

Essential Characteristics of Effective Leaders

Visionary

Effective leaders in social movements are often visionary—they have a clear, compelling idea of what they want to achieve and can articulate this vision in a way that is inspiring and accessible to others. This vision provides a roadmap for the movement and motivates participants by outlining a clear goal. Leaders like Martin Luther King Jr., with his famous "I Have a Dream" speech, exemplify the power of a strong, inclusive vision that resonates with a wide audience.

Integrity

Integrity is crucial for leaders, especially in the context of social movements. These leaders must adhere to the values they preach, as trust is the foundation of their influence. When leaders display consistency between their words and actions, it builds credibility and trust among followers, which is essential for sustaining participation and enthusiasm in a movement. Integrity also involves transparency in decision-making and actions, which helps to maintain group solidarity and commitment.

Charismatic

Charisma is a common trait among influential leaders in social movements. Charismatic leaders have the ability to draw people in and galvanize them towards a cause. Their energy and personal appeal often enhance their effectiveness in public speaking and direct actions, making their interactions with the public and their followers more impactful. The charisma of leaders like Nelson Mandela helped them to mobilize support not only from direct followers within their countries but also from international communities.

Empathetic

Effective leaders show a deep empathy towards the concerns and struggles of their followers. This empathy enables them to connect on a personal level, fostering a sense of shared fate and mutual respect. Empathy also allows leaders to understand the diverse perspectives within a movement, which is crucial for addressing internal differences and for devising strategies that accommodate various stakeholders.

Adaptive

The ability to adapt to changing circumstances is a hallmark of effective leadership in social movements. Social and political contexts can evolve rapidly, and leaders must be able to adjust their strategies and approaches in response. This adaptability can mean shifting tactics in response to opposition, overcoming unforeseen challenges, or seizing new opportunities as they arise.

Impact of Effective Leadership on Social Movements

The impact of leadership extends beyond the immediate operational successes of social movements; it also influences their long-term effectiveness and their legacy.

Mobilization of Support

Leaders mobilize support by using their vision, charisma, and credibility to inspire and recruit participants. They play a crucial role in turning passive support into active participation, which is essential for the growth and sustainability of the movement. Effective leaders are also skilled in utilizing media and other platforms to amplify their message and reach a broader audience.

Strategy and Direction

Leaders provide strategic direction to ensure that the movement remains focused and effective over time. This involves planning actions, coordinating efforts across different fronts, managing resources, and navigating the political landscape. The strategic acumen of leaders determines how well a movement can maintain its momentum, respond to challenges, and achieve its objectives.

Building Alliances

Leaders often act as representatives of their movements in the broader political and social arena. Their ability to forge alliances with other groups, stakeholders, and international bodies can be crucial for gaining the necessary support and resources needed for the movement's success. These alliances can also help legitimize the movement's goals and broaden its impact.

Legacy and Continuity

Effective leaders not only focus on the immediate goals of the movement but also on its long-term sustainability. They cultivate leadership among their followers, ensuring that the movement can continue to thrive even in their absence. This focus on developing others ensures that the movement does not revolve solely around a single charismatic leader but can sustain its momentum through a network of committed individuals.

Leadership is a critical component of social movements. The characteristics of effective leaders—such as vision, integrity, charisma, empathy, and adaptability—play significant roles in shaping the direction and success of these movements. Through their ability to inspire, strategize, mobilize, and build alliances, leaders not only drive the movement forward but also ensure its resilience and lasting impact.

ᐳᐳᐳ

"Educational empowerment goes beyond imparting knowledge; it's about changing perspectives, challenging biases, and opening minds. A truly transformative education instills the courage to question and the capacity to understand. It equips individuals not just with facts, but with the empathy to connect and the wisdom to act."

▷▷▷

TEN

THE ROLE OF EMOTIONS IN SOCIAL CHANGE

Emotions are a fundamental aspect of human psychology and play a crucial role in activism and social participation. They can drive people to take action, sustain their involvement in long-term social movements, and affect the ways in which these movements are perceived by the public. Understanding the emotional drivers behind activism is essential for anyone looking to engage in or lead social change, as it allows for more effective communication, better strategy development, and stronger connections among participants.

The Emotional Foundations of Activism

Activism is often born out of strong emotional responses to perceived injustices or societal needs. These emotions can range from anger and outrage to hope and solidarity. Each emotion carries with it distinct motivational properties that can influence the nature and sustainability of activist efforts.

Anger and Outrage

Anger is a powerful motivator. It often arises from a sense of injustice and can propel individuals into action, pushing them to address and rectify the conditions that prompted their anger. Historically, outrage at social injustices has sparked numerous movements, from the civil rights movement in the United States to more recent movements like Black Lives Matter. While anger can be an effective catalyst for drawing attention to a cause, it must be channeled appropriately to prevent it from spurring destructive actions, which can undermine the legitimacy of a movement.

Hope and Inspiration

Contrasting with anger, hope motivates individuals by focusing on the potential for positive change. Hopeful activists are driven by the belief that their actions can lead to a better future. This emotion is particularly important for sustaining long-term involvement in social movements, as it helps activists to persevere in the face of challenges and setbacks. Leaders who inspire hope, such as Mahatma Gandhi in his non-violent fight for Indian independence, can galvanize large groups of people and maintain their engagement over time.

Fear and Anxiety

Fear and anxiety can also drive social participation, particularly in movements centered around threats to community welfare, such as environmental activism driven by concerns about climate change. While these emotions can mobilize quick responses, they can also lead to burnout or paralysis if not managed properly. Effective movement leaders will recognize these risks and work to mitigate them by providing clear action steps and support for participants.

Empathy and Solidarity

Empathy involves understanding and sharing the feelings of another. This emotional connection can lead to solidarity, where individuals feel a bond with those affected by certain issues, even if they are not personally impacted. Empathy drives many to participate in movements that may not directly affect them but align with their values of justice and human rights. Solidarity is crucial for building diverse coalitions that can tackle large-scale social issues.

Emotional Intelligence in Leadership

Leaders of social movements must have high emotional intelligence to effectively harness the emotional energy of their followers and direct it towards constructive ends. This includes the ability to recognize and understand emotions in themselves and others, the capacity to handle interpersonal relationships judiciously and empathetically, and the skill to manage and regulate emotions to promote emotional and intellectual growth.

Managing Emotions

Managing the emotional climate of a movement is crucial. Leaders must create spaces where participants feel safe expressing their emotions. This may involve training in non-violent communication, establishing support networks within the movement, or using art and music to express and process feelings. Such strategies can help maintain morale and prevent burnout among activists.

Communicating with Emotional Intelligence

Effective communication within movements also requires emotional intelligence. Leaders must communicate in ways that validate the emotions of participants while guiding those emotions towards positive outcomes. This includes framing messages in ways that resonate emotionally with the audience and choosing the right times to emphasize different emotional appeals, such as switching between messages of urgency and messages of hope.

Emotions are deeply intertwined with the mechanisms of social change. They are the undercurrents that propel and sustain movements, influence the strategies employed, and affect the interaction dynamics within and outside the activist groups. Understanding and strategically managing these emotional drivers are key to effective activism. It allows leaders and participants to build stronger, more resilient movements that can withstand challenges and effect meaningful change. By leveraging the power of emotions, social change movements can more profoundly connect with individuals and communities, inspiring widespread engagement and fostering a collective commitment to transformative goals.

ᐅᐅᐅ

"Conflict is not merely an obstacle to be overcome, but a potential path to greater understanding and deeper relationships. By applying psychological strategies, we can transform conflicts from divisive to constructive forces. It's not about winning the argument, but about finding a resolution that respects all parties' needs and fosters growth."

▷▷▷

ELEVEN

BEHAVIORAL ECONOMICS AND SOCIAL POLICIES

Behavioral economics, which combines insights from psychology and economics to understand human decision-making, offers valuable tools for designing social policies that are not only effective but also efficient and responsive to human needs. Traditional economic theories often assume that people make rational decisions based on complete information and in their best interest. However, behavioral economics challenges this view by demonstrating that people are subject to biases, lack perfect self-control, and are influenced by their social environments, which can lead to decisions that deviate from what would be considered 'rational.' Understanding these behaviors is crucial in crafting policies that achieve desired outcomes by aligning with how people actually think and behave.

The Role of Behavioral Insights in Policy Making

Behavioral economics has significantly impacted the way governments and organizations design and implement policies. By acknowledging the cognitive limitations and predictable biases of individuals, policymakers can develop interventions that guide better choices without restricting freedom of choice. This approach is often referred to as "nudging," a term popularized by Richard Thaler and Cass Sunstein in their book *Nudge: Improving Decisions About Health, Wealth, and Happiness.*

Nudging for Better Outcomes

Nudges are small changes in the way choices are presented or structured that can significantly alter people's behavior in predictable ways. One classic example is the rearrangement of foods in a cafeteria to promote healthier choices; by placing fruits and vegetables at eye level or at the start of the buffet, people are more likely to pick them up. Another example is automatic enrollment in pension plans, where employees are enrolled by default but have the option to opt out. This simple change has been shown to dramatically increase participation rates in retirement savings programs.

Defaults

Defaults are powerful nudges because they play into the human tendency to stick with the pre-selected option. Policies that make beneficial behaviors the default choice (opt-out rather than opt-in) can lead to better outcomes in various domains, including organ donation and energy consumption. For example, if consumers are automatically enrolled in green energy programs but have the option to switch to a conventional source, most tend to stick with the environmentally friendly option.

Behavioral Economics in Public Health and Education

Behavioral insights have also been effectively applied in public health and education, areas where traditional interventions sometimes fall short due to a lack of consideration for human behavior.

Public Health

In public health, understanding the factors that influence unhealthy behavior can lead to more effective interventions. For example, smoking cessation programs that utilize text message reminders can take advantage of the immediacy and personal nature of mobile communications to nudge individuals towards quitting. Similarly, reducing the size of plates and glasses can nudge people to consume less, a simple yet effective intervention based on the insight that people often consume more when given larger servings, regardless of hunger levels.

Education

In education, behavioral economics can help in designing programs that increase student engagement and improve learning outcomes. For instance, sending parents simple and actionable messages about ways to support their child's education can enhance engagement in learning activities at home. Another approach is using commitment devices, such as study plans that make students commit to specific goals each week, which can improve academic discipline.

Behavioral Economics and Financial Policies

Financial behavior is another area where behavioral economics has had a profound impact. Policies designed to promote savings and investment behaviors can benefit from insights into how people perceive money and make financial decisions.

Saving and Spending

Programs that help individuals save more effectively often use techniques such as pre-commitment strategies, where people commit to saving a certain amount of money that is automatically deducted from their wages. For spending, reminders about the long-term costs of debt can discourage excessive credit card use by exploiting loss aversion—an inherent tendency to strongly prefer avoiding losses to acquiring equivalent gains.

Overcoming Limitations and Challenges

While behavioral economics offers powerful tools for policy design, it also comes with limitations. Critics argue that nudges may be manipulative and infringe on individual autonomy. Moreover, behavioral interventions can sometimes lead to unintended consequences if not carefully implemented. Policymakers must ensure that these strategies are transparent and that they respect individual freedom and promote welfare.

Behavioral economics provides a rich set of tools that can enhance the effectiveness of social policies by aligning them more closely with human behavior. By understanding and leveraging the predictable ways in which people make decisions, policymakers can design interventions that promote healthier, wealthier, and happier societies. These insights are especially valuable in areas where traditional economic and public policy interventions have failed to produce desired outcomes, offering a fresh perspective and new tools to tackle persistent challenges.

ᗏᗏᗏ

"Artificial intelligence and virtual realities are redefining what it means to interact and connect. As we navigate this new frontier, social psychologists must ensure these technologies enhance human welfare and social cohesion, not undermine them. Our challenge is to integrate these tools thoughtfully, preserving the essence of human connection."

ᐅᐅᐅ

TWELVE
Technology and Social Impact

Technology has become a powerful force in modern society, fundamentally transforming how we communicate, work, and engage with the world around us. Its role in facilitating social change and enhancing engagement in civic activities cannot be overstated. As digital tools and platforms become increasingly embedded in daily life, they offer unique opportunities to drive social progress and foster a more connected and informed public.

Leveraging Technology for Social Change

Digital Communication Platforms

One of the most significant impacts of technology on social change is through digital communication platforms, such as social media, blogs, and podcasts. These platforms allow for the rapid dissemination of information and ideas, enabling movements and causes to gain visibility and momentum quickly. For instance, social media played a pivotal role in the Arab Spring, where it was used to organize protests, spread awareness, and bring international attention to the struggles for democracy in various countries. Similarly, platforms like Twitter and Facebook have become vital tools for movements such as #MeToo and Black Lives Matter, providing spaces for sharing stories and mobilizing support.

Crowdfunding and Fundraising

Technology has also revolutionized fundraising and resource mobilization. Crowdfunding platforms like Kickstarter, GoFundMe, and Indiegogo allow individuals and organizations to raise funds directly from the public for social projects, emergency relief, and community initiatives. This democratization of funding enables more ideas and projects to come to fruition, particularly those that might not attract traditional funding sources. Additionally, these platforms often provide transparency about how funds are used, increasing donor confidence and accountability.

Data and Analytics for Social Good

The use of big data and analytics in social change initiatives offers profound insights into complex issues, enabling more targeted and effective interventions. Organizations can use data to monitor and evaluate the impact of their programs, optimize resource allocation, and identify needs and trends within communities. For example, during natural disasters, real-time data analysis can help coordinate response efforts more efficiently, ensuring that aid reaches those most in need quickly. In the public health sector, data analytics is used to track disease outbreaks and to optimize the distribution of healthcare resources.

Enhancing Civic Engagement and Participation

Technology not only supports the mechanics of social change but also enhances civic engagement by making participation more accessible and engaging.

E-Governance and Digital Democracy

Technological innovations have facilitated greater transparency and interaction between governments and citizens through e-governance platforms. These platforms allow citizens to access services, communicate with officials, and participate in decision-making processes online. In Estonia, for example, e-residency programs enable people worldwide to start and manage businesses governed by Estonian laws, regardless of their geographical location. Additionally, digital voting systems can increase participation in elections, making it easier and faster for citizens to exercise their democratic rights.

Social Media as a Tool for Civic Awareness

Social media platforms are powerful tools for raising awareness and fostering dialogue around civic issues. They enable individuals to share information, discuss and debate issues, and organize around causes. The interactive nature of social media also allows for greater accountability of public figures and institutions, as citizens can directly engage with them in public forums.

Educational Technology

Educational technologies, including online courses, mobile learning apps, and interactive educational games, have made learning more accessible and engaging for people of all ages. These technologies can be particularly powerful in regions with limited educational infrastructure, providing remote learning opportunities that were previously unimaginable. Moreover, they offer platforms for civic education, teaching users about their rights, responsibilities, and how to engage effectively in civic life.

Overcoming Challenges and Ensuring Inclusivity

While technology offers numerous opportunities for social change, it also poses challenges such as digital divides, privacy concerns, and the potential for misinformation. Addressing these challenges requires thoughtful policy-making, robust technological safeguards, and ongoing education to ensure that technological advancements benefit all segments of society.

Technology holds immense potential to promote social change and enhance civic engagement. By harnessing the power of digital tools and platforms, individuals and organizations can drive progress in unprecedented ways. From improving communication and mobilizing resources to enhancing participation in democratic processes, technology offers pathways to a more engaged and informed society. However, the benefits of technology must be tempered with a commitment to addressing the associated risks and ensuring that its potential is harnessed ethically and inclusively.

 design

"Forgiveness is not just an act of mercy towards another, but a profound gift to oneself. By embracing forgiveness, we release ourselves from the shackles of resentment and open our hearts to healing and peace. It is often the first step toward genuine reconciliation and lasting change."

ᐅᐅᐅ

THIRTEEN

ENVIRONMENTAL PSYCHOLOGY

Environmental psychology is a field that examines the interplay between individuals and their surroundings, offering crucial insights into how people perceive, interact with, and impact the environment. This understanding is pivotal for developing effective strategies to promote sustainable behavior and mitigate environmental issues such as climate change, pollution, and biodiversity loss. By exploring the psychological factors that influence environmental behavior, we can devise interventions that encourage sustainable practices and foster a greater connection between individuals and the natural world.

Understanding Environmental Perceptions

The way people perceive the environment and their beliefs about their personal impact play a critical role in shaping their behaviors. Environmental awareness does not automatically lead to action, often due to a lack of personal connection or the perception that one's actions cannot significantly influence global issues like climate change. Environmental psychology seeks to bridge this gap by enhancing individuals' perceptions of their personal efficacy in affecting environmental change.

Personal and Social Identity

A person's identity and values can significantly influence their environmental attitudes and behaviors. For instance, individuals who strongly identify with environmental movements or who see themselves as part of a community concerned about the environment are more likely to engage in behaviors that they perceive as environmentally friendly. Social norms also play a crucial role; when sustainable practices become seen as the norm within a community, individuals are more likely to conform to these practices.

Psychological Distance

Psychological distance refers to the way people disassociate themselves from the consequences of environmental issues, which are often perceived as distant in time or space. This can reduce the urgency of taking action. Reducing psychological distance—by making the impacts of environmental issues more immediate and personal—can increase engagement and willingness to act. Visual imagery, simulations, and personal narratives about the effects of environmental degradation can help make these issues feel more concrete and urgent.

Promoting Sustainable Behavior

Environmental psychology provides insights into various strategies that can effectively promote sustainability. These strategies focus on altering individual behaviors and making broader systemic changes.

Encouraging Conservation Behaviors

Simple interventions such as providing feedback on energy use can significantly influence conservation efforts. For example, when households are given data about their electricity consumption in comparison to their neighbors, they often adjust their behavior to be more in line with or better than the norm. Additionally, prompting individuals with reminders to perform environmentally friendly actions, such as recycling or turning off lights, can also be effective.

Changing Habits

Many environmentally harmful behaviors are habitual and performed without much conscious thought. Changing these habits requires creating new cues and rewards that encourage sustainable actions. For instance, making recycling bins more accessible and visible than trash bins can cue the more environmentally friendly behavior of recycling.

Designing Sustainable Environments

The design of physical spaces can significantly influence environmental behavior. For example, buildings designed with energy efficiency in mind not only reduce energy consumption but also subtly encourage occupants to think more about sustainability. Urban planning that promotes green spaces and supports walking, cycling, and public transportation can reduce car usage and its associated environmental impact.

Addressing Environmental Attitudes and Mental Health

The psychological impact of environmental issues, particularly large-scale problems like climate change, can lead to feelings of stress, helplessness, and eco-anxiety. Understanding and addressing these feelings is crucial in maintaining public engagement in environmental actions.

Building Resilience

Supporting community resilience can mitigate the psychological impacts of environmental issues. Community-based initiatives that involve individuals in local environmental projects, such as community gardens or cleanup days, can enhance social cohesion and empower individuals by giving them active roles in environmental stewardship.

Promoting Ecotherapy

Ecotherapy, which involves direct engagement with nature, has been shown to reduce stress, improve mood, and enhance psychological well-being. By promoting regular interaction with the natural environment, individuals can strengthen their emotional connection to the environment, which can encourage more mindful and sustainable living.

Environmental psychology offers vital insights into how individuals and communities interact with their environments. By applying these insights, we can better design interventions that promote sustainable behavior, enhance the psychological well-being of communities, and foster a deeper connection with the natural world. Understanding the psychological dimensions of environmental issues is essential for addressing the environmental challenges of our time, ensuring that efforts to promote sustainability are as effective and holistic as possible.

ᑭᑭᑭ

"As environmental challenges mount, the role of psychology in fostering an ecological consciousness becomes ever more critical. Understanding the emotional and cognitive barriers to pro-environmental behavior can lead to more effective advocacy and action. It's not just about saving the planet—it's about aligning our beliefs with our actions."

ᐅᐅᐅ

FOURTEEN

EDUCATION FOR EMPOWERMENT

Education is a powerful tool for empowerment, capable of leveling the playing field and providing individuals with the skills and knowledge they need to improve their lives and influence society. Beyond imparting technical skills and information, education that fosters social equity and empowerment also addresses psychological and sociocultural factors that influence learning and personal development. Understanding and applying psychological approaches in educational settings can significantly enhance the effectiveness of these initiatives, promoting not only individual growth but also societal change.

Fostering a Growth Mindset

One of the most influential psychological concepts in education today is the growth mindset, developed by psychologist Carol Dweck. This approach distinguishes between fixed and growth mindsets; individuals with a fixed mindset believe that abilities such as intelligence are static and unchangeable, while those with a growth mindset believe that abilities can be developed through effort, learning, and persistence. Educators who encourage a growth mindset in students foster an environment where challenges are embraced, failures are seen as opportunities for growth, and persistence is developed. This mindset is particularly empowering in educational contexts as it helps students from diverse backgrounds believe in their potential to learn and succeed, regardless of their starting point.

Building Self-Efficacy in Learning

Self-efficacy, a term coined by psychologist Albert Bandura, refers to an individual's belief in their capability to achieve specific outcomes. In education, promoting self-efficacy involves providing students with tasks that they can successfully complete, which in turn boosts their confidence in their abilities. This can be particularly transformative for students from marginalized groups who may not have had many opportunities to succeed in traditional learning environments. Strategies to enhance self-efficacy include setting clear and achievable goals, providing constructive feedback, and celebrating small wins to reinforce students' sense of accomplishment.

Culturally Responsive Teaching

Culturally responsive teaching is an educational approach that recognizes the importance of including students' cultural references in all aspects of learning. This approach understands that students bring unique cultural strengths and by incorporating these into the learning process, educators can enhance students' academic outcomes and personal growth. Culturally responsive teaching not only addresses educational content but also the pedagogy, relationships, and classroom environment. It empowers students by valuing and leveraging the diversity they bring to their education, making learning more relevant and effective.

Emotional Intelligence in Education

Emotional intelligence, which involves understanding and managing one's emotions and empathizing with others, is another critical component of education for empowerment. By integrating emotional intelligence into the curriculum, educators can help students develop key skills such as self-awareness, self-regulation, motivation, empathy, and social skills. These skills are essential for personal empowerment as they enhance students' ability to navigate social complexities, build and maintain interpersonal relationships, and make informed decisions. Education programs that incorporate emotional intelligence training can contribute significantly to reducing bullying, enhancing student relationships, and creating more supportive learning environments.

Cooperative and Collaborative Learning

Cooperative learning is an instructional strategy that involves students working together on common tasks or learning goals. This approach is based on the idea that learning is inherently social and that significant engagement increases retention and understanding. Collaborative learning models promote a sense of community and shared responsibility, which can empower students by giving them a more active role in their education. These approaches also teach important life skills such as communication, conflict resolution, and teamwork, which are essential for both personal success and active citizenship.

Problem-Based Learning

Problem-based learning (PBL) is an educational approach that uses complex and real-world problems as the starting point for learning. PBL develops critical thinking, problem-solving skills, and the ability to transfer knowledge to new situations, empowering students to handle real-life challenges. This method is particularly effective in promoting empowerment as it encourages learners to take control of their learning process, fosters independence, and provides skills that are directly applicable beyond the classroom.

Psychological approaches to education play a crucial role in promoting social equity and empowerment. By fostering a growth mindset, building self-efficacy, incorporating culturally responsive teaching, integrating emotional intelligence, facilitating cooperative learning, and implementing problem-based learning, educational systems can not only enhance academic achievement but also empower individuals to become active, engaged, and informed participants in society. These strategies not only transform individuals but also have the potential to effect broader social change, as empowered individuals are more likely to advocate for themselves and others, contributing to a more equitable world.

ᐅᐅᐅ

"The anonymity of the internet can be a double-edged sword—liberating us to express ourselves freely but also tempting us towards incivility. Navigating this digital landscape requires a new kind of literacy, one that embraces empathy and accountability as keystones of online interaction. Let us strive to be as compassionate in our virtual worlds as we are in our real ones."

ppp

FIFTEEN

Health Psychology and Community Wellbeing

Health psychology and community wellbeing are deeply intertwined fields that focus on enhancing the health of individuals and communities through psychological principles. This integration of psychology and public health provides a comprehensive approach to tackling health issues, emphasizing both prevention and intervention strategies. By understanding how psychological factors influence health behaviors and outcomes, public health initiatives can be designed more effectively to promote overall wellbeing.

The Role of Health Psychology

Health psychology primarily focuses on how biological, psychological, and social factors affect health and illness. Its role in public health is to understand and intervene in the psychological processes that underpin health behaviors. This includes studying how people respond to illness, how they make health-related decisions, and how they manage and overcome health challenges.

Behavioral Medicine

A key component of health psychology is behavioral medicine, which applies psychological knowledge and techniques to the treatment of physical illness. This approach recognizes that many illnesses are preventable and that behaviors such as smoking, diet, and physical inactivity significantly impact health. Behavioral medicine programs often involve interventions to change these behaviors, incorporating techniques from cognitive-behavioral therapy, motivational interviewing, and stress reduction.

Psychoneuroimmunology

Another important area is psychoneuroimmunology, which explores how the mind influences immune function. Research in this field has shown that stress, depression, and other psychological factors can affect the body's immune system, leading to an increased risk of conditions like infections and autoimmune diseases. Understanding these connections can help in designing interventions that not only target the body but also the mind.

Community Wellbeing and Public Health Initiatives

Community wellbeing is a broader concept that encompasses the overall psychological, physical, and social health of a community. It is influenced by a range of factors, including economic stability, environmental conditions, and social relationships. Public health initiatives aimed at improving community wellbeing often focus on enhancing these factors through community-wide strategies.

Social Determinants of Health

Public health recognizes that health disparities are often rooted in social determinants of health—conditions in the environments where people are born, live, learn, work, and age. These conditions affect a wide range of health and quality-of-life outcomes. Health psychologists work within public health to address these determinants by advocating for policies that improve living conditions, access to healthcare, education, and employment.

Community-Based Interventions

Community-based interventions are collaborative efforts aimed at enhancing the resources available within a community to improve overall health. These interventions might include creating safer neighborhood environments, providing more accessible healthcare services, or developing educational programs that address specific community health needs. By involving the community in these efforts, these interventions not only improve health outcomes but also strengthen community bonds and support networks.

Integrating Mental Health in Public Health

Mental health is an essential component of public health, yet it is often overlooked in public health initiatives. Integrating mental health services with other community health efforts can lead to better overall health outcomes.

Reducing Stigma

One major barrier to mental health care is stigma. Health psychology plays a crucial role in combating mental health stigma through education and by promoting more positive attitudes towards mental health conditions. Effective strategies include public speaking events, workshops, and media campaigns that provide accurate information and counteract common myths about mental illness.

Holistic Health Programs

Programs that consider both physical and mental health are more effective at improving overall wellbeing. For example, an exercise program for older adults can include elements of social support to help reduce loneliness, which is known to have a negative impact on mental health. Similarly, weight loss programs can be more effective when they include components that address stress management and emotional eating.

Challenges and Future Directions

While the integration of health psychology and public health has led to significant improvements in community wellbeing, challenges remain. These include funding limitations, the complexity of measuring psychological and social outcomes, and the need for more comprehensive training for health professionals in the psychological aspects of health care.

Health psychology and community wellbeing are crucial aspects of public health that address the psychological factors influencing health behaviors and outcomes. By combining efforts in these areas, it is possible to create more effective and holistic health interventions. Moving forward, it is essential that public health initiatives continue to integrate psychological knowledge and techniques to foster environments that support both the mental and physical health of all community members.

ppp

"Behavioral economics offers a lens through which
to view the subtle nudges that influence decision-
making. By understanding these dynamics, we can
design interventions that gently steer people
towards healthier, more sustainable choices. It's
about making the better choice the easier choice."

▷▷▷

SIXTEEN
CONFLICT RESOLUTION

Conflict resolution is a vital area of psychology that deals with the ways in which individuals and groups manage disputes and disagreements. By applying psychological strategies, it is possible to transform conflicts into opportunities for growth and development, promoting peace and understanding. Understanding the psychological underpinnings of conflict and the methods for resolving it can significantly improve personal relationships, workplace dynamics, and international relations.

Understanding the Nature of Conflict

Conflict arises from differences between individuals or groups and can manifest as disagreements over values, motivations, perceptions, ideas, or desires. At its core, conflict is often about basic needs such as security, recognition, and respect, not just surface issues. Psychological strategies for conflict resolution thus start with a deep understanding of these underlying needs and the emotions involved.

Emotional Intelligence in Conflict Resolution

Emotional intelligence, the ability to understand and manage one's own emotions and empathize with others, plays a crucial role in conflict resolution. High emotional intelligence can help individuals navigate the complexities of conflict more effectively by allowing them to:

Recognize and understand their own emotional responses to conflict.

Understand the emotions of others involved in the conflict, fostering empathy and communication.

Regulate their emotions to maintain a calm, respectful approach to discussions.

Psychological Strategies for Resolving Conflicts

Active Listening

Active listening is more than just hearing words; it involves understanding the message being communicated and showing respect for the speaker's perspective. This method involves listening not only for what is said but also for what is left unsaid or only partially expressed. Techniques include:

Paraphrasing what has been said to show understanding.

Asking open-ended questions to clarify points.

Expressing empathy through verbal and non-verbal cues.

Assertive Communication

Assertive communication is a key psychological strategy that involves expressing one's thoughts, feelings, and needs in a direct, honest, and respectful way. It stands in contrast to passive or aggressive communication, which can exacerbate conflicts. Assertive communicators use "I" statements (e.g., "I feel frustrated when meetings start late because it disrupts my schedule") rather than blaming or accusatory statements, which can help reduce defensive responses.

Negotiation Techniques

Negotiation is a process where two or more parties with differing needs and goals discuss an issue to find a mutually acceptable solution. Effective negotiation involves several psychological techniques:

Preparation: Understanding one's needs and the needs of the other party.

Problem-solving: Looking for solutions that satisfy both parties' core needs.

Compromise: Finding a middle ground where concessions are made by all parties.

Mediation

Mediation involves a neutral third party who helps disputants reach an agreement. The mediator facilitates communication, helping parties find common ground and resolve their differences. Psychological principles applied in mediation focus on defusing tensions, encouraging mutual respect, and fostering a cooperative rather than adversarial mindset.

Psychological De-escalation

De-escalation techniques are crucial in situations where emotions run high. These techniques involve:

Reducing the intensity of an emotional reaction.

Encouraging a shift from emotional to more rational thinking.

Using calming techniques such as deep breathing or breaks in the discussion.

The Role of Forgiveness and Reconciliation

Forgiveness is a powerful psychological tool in conflict resolution, involving a conscious decision to let go of resentment and thoughts of revenge. The act of forgiving can reduce the stress that comes with conflict and lead to healthier relationships. Reconciliation goes a step further, seeking to rebuild trust and return to a positive relationship. Psychological approaches to fostering forgiveness and reconciliation include:

Empathy development: Encouraging individuals to see things from the other person's perspective.

Dialogue: Facilitating open discussions about grievances and hurts.

Commitment to future relationship health: Making explicit agreements to change behaviors and interactions.

Challenges in Conflict Resolution

Despite the best psychological strategies, not all conflicts can be easily resolved. Challenges may arise due to deeply entrenched beliefs, power imbalances, or previous traumas. Additionally, cultural differences can affect communication styles and perceptions of conflict, requiring culturally sensitive approaches.

Conflict resolution requires a comprehensive understanding of the psychological aspects of human behavior. By employing strategies such as active listening, assertive communication, negotiation, mediation, and psychological de-escalation, individuals and groups can resolve disputes effectively and promote peace. Additionally, fostering forgiveness and reconciliation can lead to more enduring solutions and healthier relationships. As conflicts are inevitable in human interactions, mastering these psychological strategies is essential for creating more harmonious interactions at all levels of society.

ᐵᐵᐵ

"Culturally responsive teaching not only
acknowledges diversity but celebrates it, creating
an educational environment where all students can
thrive. This approach doesn't just teach content—it
builds understanding and respect among students
from various backgrounds. In this rich soil, new
ideas and innovations can flourish."

ᐯᐯᐯ

SEVENTEEN

SOCIAL PSYCHOLOGY OF THE INTERNET

The social psychology of the internet explores how digital environments influence individual and group behaviors, shaping interactions both online and offline. The internet, as a pervasive force in modern life, has unique attributes that significantly affect social behaviors and attitudes, including anonymity, accessibility, and the ability to connect with a vast network of people. Understanding these influences is crucial for grasping the broader impacts of digital technology on society.

The Internet as a Social Space

The internet has created new social spaces that function differently from traditional physical environments. These spaces allow for interactions that can be anonymous or pseudonymous, providing users with opportunities to express themselves in ways they might avoid in face-to-face settings. This can lead to both positive and negative outcomes, influencing real-world behaviors and societal norms.

Anonymity and Disinhibition

Online anonymity can lead to a disinhibition effect, where individuals share their thoughts or exhibit behaviors more freely than they might in person. This can encourage openness and honesty, and allow for the exploration of identity in a seemingly low-risk environment. However, it can also lead to negative behaviors, such as cyberbullying or the spread of misinformation, as the lack of accountability and immediate social feedback removes many of the social and ethical constraints observed in face-to-face interactions.

Echo Chambers and Polarization

The internet facilitates the formation of echo chambers—online spaces where individuals are exposed primarily to viewpoints that align with their own. Algorithms used by social media platforms often enhance this effect by feeding users content that they are likely to engage with, based on their past behavior. This can intensify beliefs and contribute to polarization, as individuals become more entrenched in their views and less exposed to differing perspectives. Such polarization can translate into offline behaviors, affecting political and social divides in the real world.

Influence on Identity and Self-Concept

The internet offers vast opportunities for self-presentation and identity exploration. Users can curate their online personas, highlight certain aspects of their lives, and downplay others. This can influence self-concept and self-esteem.

Online Identity as Social Currency

On platforms like Instagram and Twitter, the online self can become a form of social currency. How individuals present themselves online can affect their social standing both online and offline. The pursuit of validation, in the form of likes and comments, can lead to an increased focus on external validation rather than self-acceptance, impacting real-world behaviors and mental health.

Virtual Communities and Social Support

The internet also allows for the formation of virtual communities that can offer social support that might not be available offline. For individuals with rare diseases, unique hobbies, or specific interests, the internet can be a vital source of connection and support. These communities can empower individuals, enhance their knowledge and coping strategies, and influence their offline behaviors in positive ways.

The Internet's Impact on Real-World Behavior

Online interactions can directly influence offline behaviors through various mechanisms, such as social learning, normalization of behaviors, and the spread of cultural norms.

Social Learning

The internet is a powerful tool for social learning, where users can observe and model behaviors learned from others online. This can be beneficial, as in the case of educational content or pro-social behaviors shared via YouTube or other platforms. However, it can also lead to the spread of harmful behaviors, such as risky challenges or unhealthy lifestyle habits.

Normalization of Behaviors

Behaviors observed online can become normalized through repeated exposure. This normalization process can influence real-world behaviors by altering perceptions of what is typical or acceptable. For example, exposure to aggressive online rhetoric can desensitize individuals to hostility, potentially increasing aggressive behavior in offline settings.

Cultural Exchange and Globalization

The internet accelerates cultural exchange and globalization, impacting behaviors by exposing individuals to a broader array of cultural norms and practices. This can lead to greater cultural understanding and tolerance but also cultural homogenization, where dominant cultures overshadow local customs.

Addressing Online Influence

Understanding the social psychology of the internet is essential for addressing its influence on society. This includes creating strategies to mitigate harmful behaviors and enhance the benefits of online interactions. Policymakers, educators, and individuals must navigate these challenges by promoting digital literacy, encouraging ethical online behavior, and fostering an internet environment that supports healthy social interaction.

The internet significantly influences real-world behaviors and attitudes through mechanisms like anonymity, echo chambers, and the opportunity for identity exploration. By studying the social psychology of the internet, we can better understand these phenomena and work towards a digital society that enhances personal and societal well-being.

ᘖᘖᘖ

"In an age where information is plentiful but wisdom is scarce, the role of educators extends beyond the classroom. They are not just teachers but guides, tasked with helping students navigate a world teeming with complexity and contradiction. Their greatest gift is not to provide answers, but to inspire questions."

ᗺᗺᗺ

EIGHTEEN

VOLUNTEERISM AND SOCIAL RESPONSIBILITY

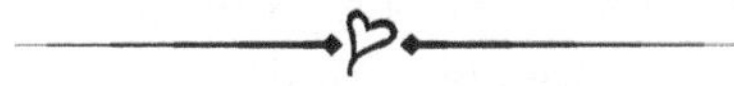

Volunteerism is a powerful force in society, reflecting a complex interplay of altruistic, social, and personal motivations. Understanding the psychological drivers behind why people volunteer, as well as the impacts of their actions on communities, is crucial for nurturing a culture of social responsibility and strengthening community ties.

The Psychology of Volunteerism

Volunteerism is often seen as a selfless act of helping others, but the motivations behind it can be diverse, involving both self-oriented and other-oriented factors.

Altruism

Altruism, or the desire to help others without expecting something in return, is a significant motivator for many volunteers. This can stem from empathy, where individuals feel a strong emotional response to the needs of others, compelling them to take action to alleviate their distress. Psychological theories such as the empathy-altruism hypothesis suggest that empathic concern directly correlates with altruistic behavior, indicating that the more one empathizes with the sufferings of others, the more likely one is to help.

Personal Growth and Well-being

Volunteering is also motivated by personal benefits, including emotional satisfaction, personal growth, and skill development. Engaging in volunteer work can enhance one's sense of purpose and self-esteem, providing psychological well-being that goes beyond the immediate benefits of the activities performed. Furthermore, volunteering provides opportunities for learning new skills, networking, and enhancing one's resume, which can also serve as significant motivators.

Social Influence

Social norms and influences play a crucial role in promoting volunteerism. Individuals are more likely to engage in volunteering if they are part of a social network that values and engages in community service. The desire for social approval and to maintain a positive self-image in the eyes of others can also drive volunteerism. Additionally, being part of a volunteer group satisfies basic social needs, such as belonging and connectedness, reinforcing continued engagement in volunteer activities.

Impact of Volunteerism on Communities

Volunteerism has a profound impact on communities, contributing to their development and resilience. Volunteers often provide essential services that improve the quality of life within communities, from educational support and healthcare services to disaster response and environmental conservation.

Building Social Capital

Volunteers play a significant role in building social capital—the networks of relationships among people who live and work in a particular society, enabling that society to function effectively. Volunteerism fosters trust and reciprocity among community members, which are essential for cohesive communities. By participating in volunteer activities, individuals connect with others, build trust, and develop a sense of mutual obligation, strengthening the social fabric of the community.

Enhancing Community Resilience

Volunteerism enhances community resilience by enabling communities to respond to and recover from adverse situations, such as natural disasters, economic downturns, or social unrest. Volunteers provide immediate relief efforts and long-term recovery initiatives, essential for rebuilding and strengthening affected communities.

Promoting Civic Engagement

Engaging in volunteer activities can increase individuals' civic engagement by raising awareness about societal issues and encouraging participation in community decision-making processes. Volunteers often gain a deeper understanding of the challenges within their communities, which can motivate them to advocate for and implement changes beyond the scope of their initial volunteer activities.

Challenges in Sustaining Volunteerism

Despite its benefits, sustaining volunteer involvement over time can be challenging. Volunteer burnout, lack of resources, and inadequate recognition of volunteers' efforts can diminish their motivation and ability to continue volunteering.

Addressing Volunteer Burnout

Burnout among volunteers can occur due to emotional exhaustion, particularly when volunteering involves dealing with challenging issues such as homelessness, poverty, or illness. Providing adequate support and ensuring that volunteers have the resources they need to perform their tasks effectively can help mitigate these challenges.

Recognizing and Rewarding Volunteers

Recognition is also a critical factor in sustaining volunteerism. Formal and informal recognition practices, such as awards, thank-you events, and public acknowledgment, can significantly boost volunteer morale and encourage continued participation.

Volunteerism is driven by a mixture of altruistic, personal, and social motivations and has a significant impact on community well-being and cohesion. By understanding these psychological drivers and the benefits of volunteerism, communities can better support and engage volunteers in meaningful ways, thereby enhancing the collective well-being and resilience of society.

 DDD

"Community-based interventions are most effective when they harness the existing strengths and resources of the community. By empowering communities to take the lead in addressing their challenges, we ensure solutions are not only implemented but sustained. Ownership is the key to transformation."

ᐅᐅᐅ

NINETEEN

FUTURE TRENDS IN SOCIAL PSYCHOLOGY

As we look to the future, social psychology will continue to play a crucial role in understanding and addressing the challenges that arise in increasingly complex social environments. The discipline is poised to tackle a range of emerging trends and issues, from technological advancements to global crises, all of which will significantly impact human behavior and social structures. This examination of potential future trends in social psychology not only highlights upcoming challenges but also proposes strategies for effectively managing these dynamics to foster positive social change.

Technological Influence on Social Behavior

One of the most significant trends that social psychology will need to address is the ongoing influence of technology on human behavior. The digital revolution has transformed the way people interact, form relationships, and perceive themselves and the world around them.

Virtual Reality and Augmented Reality

As virtual reality (VR) and augmented reality (AR) technologies become more sophisticated and accessible, they will increasingly affect social interactions and the psychological experiences of users. Social psychologists will need to study the impacts of immersive digital environments on concepts like self-identity, empathy, and social cognition. For instance, VR has the potential to be used as a powerful tool in empathy training, allowing individuals to experience life from the perspective of someone from a completely different background or with different life experiences.

Artificial Intelligence and Social Norms

Artificial intelligence (AI) is another area that will increasingly intersect with social psychology. AI systems are starting to shape social norms and influence decision-making processes in areas ranging from judicial decisions to healthcare. Social psychologists will need to explore how these technologies affect human autonomy, ethical standards, and interpersonal relationships, as well as how they can be used to enhance human well-being responsibly.

Environmental Challenges and Human Behavior

With global environmental changes escalating, social psychology must address how individuals and communities respond to issues like climate change, resource scarcity, and natural disasters.

Promoting Sustainable Behavior

Understanding the psychological barriers to pro-environmental behaviors is critical. Social psychologists will increasingly work on developing interventions that can effectively change environmental attitudes and behaviors on a large scale. This might involve using psychological insights to design better public policy that encourages sustainable practices or developing community programs that shift social norms toward more environmentally friendly practices.

Psychological Resilience in the Face of Climate Change

As environmental crises become more frequent, social psychology will also need to focus on resilience—how individuals and communities can psychologically cope with and adapt to increased environmental stressors. Research will likely focus on developing strategies that help communities recover from environmental disasters and adapt to new environmental realities.

Social Inequalities and Justice

As societal awareness of various forms of inequality (such as racial, gender, and economic) increases, social psychology will play a crucial role in understanding and addressing these issues.

Intersectionality and Social Identity

Future research in social psychology will likely emphasize a more nuanced understanding of intersectionality—the ways in which various forms of inequality intersect and affect individuals' experiences. This will involve studying the complex ways in which identity, power, and privilege interact in shaping social attitudes and behaviors.

Addressing Systemic Inequalities

Social psychologists will also be instrumental in developing and evaluating interventions aimed at reducing systemic inequalities. This will involve not only identifying the psychological foundations of prejudice and discrimination but also designing educational programs and community interventions that promote greater social justice.

Preparing for Future Challenges

To effectively meet these future challenges, social psychology must evolve in several key ways:

Interdisciplinary Collaboration

Social psychologists will need to collaborate more extensively with experts from other fields, such as environmental science, public policy, technology, and neuroscience, to develop comprehensive solutions to complex social issues.

Global Perspective

Taking a more global perspective will be crucial, as many of the challenges social psychology will address are global in scope. This will involve cross-cultural research to understand how social psychological processes might vary across different cultural contexts and how interventions can be adapted to be culturally sensitive.

Ethical Considerations

As social psychologists increasingly intervene in important societal issues, ethical considerations will become even more critical. Researchers will need to navigate the ethical implications of their work carefully, ensuring that interventions respect individual rights and contribute positively to societal well-being.

The future of social psychology promises significant opportunities to contribute to understanding and improving the human condition. By anticipating future trends and challenges, social psychologists can prepare to make substantial contributions to individual well-being and societal health, particularly in the face of rapid social and technological change.

ᐅᐅᐅ

"The pursuit of social justice is a complex journey that requires courage, resilience, and an unwavering commitment to equality. Social psychologists play a vital role in this journey, offering insights into how to dismantle barriers and foster an inclusive society. Every step taken is a step towards a fairer world."

ᚦᚦᚦ

TWENTY

CREATING LASTING CHANGE

Creating lasting change in communities is a multifaceted endeavor that requires a deep understanding of social dynamics, individual behaviors, and the systemic structures that influence them. This conclusion draws together key insights from the various fields of social psychology discussed throughout the text and outlines actionable steps that readers can take to foster positive transformations within their own communities.

Integrating Insights from Social Psychology

Social psychology offers invaluable tools for understanding how individuals think, influence others, and are influenced by their social environment. By leveraging these insights, individuals and organizations can design interventions that are both effective and sustainable.

Understanding Human Behavior

Effective community change initiatives begin with a clear understanding of the factors that drive human behavior. This includes recognizing the roles of cognitive biases, social influences, and emotional responses in shaping behaviors. For instance, campaigns promoting public health can benefit from social proof by showcasing widespread community support for healthy behaviors.

The Power of Social Norms

Social norms are the unwritten rules that govern behavior in a group. Understanding and influencing these norms can lead to profound changes in community behavior. For example, if recycling becomes a community norm, individual members are more likely to participate in recycling programs without the need for coercion.

The Role of Leadership

Effective leadership is crucial for initiating and sustaining community change. Leaders who are respected within the community can motivate others, mediate conflicts, and guide collective efforts towards common goals. Leadership training should, therefore, be an integral part of community development programs to ensure that leaders can effectively manage group dynamics and inspire action.

Steps for Creating Lasting Change

To transform insights into action, community members, leaders, and organizations can follow a series of steps designed to create impactful and lasting change.

Step 1: Assess Community Needs and Resources

The first step in initiating change is to conduct a thorough assessment of the community's needs and resources. This involves identifying the issues that are most important to community members, as well as the assets that the community can leverage in addressing these issues. Tools such as surveys, focus groups, and community forums can be useful in gathering this information.

Step 2: Build Collaborative Networks

Change is rarely the work of a single individual or organization. Building networks of collaborators who share a commitment to specific community goals can amplify efforts and pool resources effectively. These networks might include local businesses, schools, nonprofits, and government agencies, each bringing unique skills and perspectives to the table.

Step 3: Develop and Implement Action Plans

With a clear understanding of community needs and a network of collaborators in place, the next step is to develop a detailed action plan. This plan should outline specific, measurable objectives, the strategies that will be used to achieve these objectives, and the metrics that will be used to evaluate success. Implementation should be monitored regularly to adjust strategies as needed based on what is working and what is not.

Step 4: Foster Community Engagement and Ownership

For change to be sustainable, the community must take ownership of the initiatives. This can be achieved by involving community members in every stage of the planning and implementation process. Providing education and training can empower community members, increase their commitment to the change effort, and develop local leaders.

Step 5: Evaluate and Scale Up

Continuous evaluation is key to understanding the impact of any initiative and to making necessary adjustments. Evaluation should consider both the outcomes of the project and the processes involved in its implementation. Successful strategies can then be scaled up to have a broader impact or adapted to other contexts within the community.

Creating lasting change requires a thoughtful approach that combines an understanding of social psychology with practical action. By applying the insights from social psychology, communities can design more effective interventions that are tailored to the unique needs and dynamics of their members. Ultimately, the goal is to foster environments where positive change is not only initiated but sustained, leading to healthier, more vibrant, and more equitable communities.

"Volunteerism enriches both the giver and the receiver, creating cycles of kindness that strengthen our social fabric. It is an expression of the fundamental human desire to make a difference, a testament to the impact that individual actions can have on collective welfare. Let each act of volunteerism ignite a spark of generosity across communities."

ᗡᗡᗡ

TWENTY-ONE
SUMMARY

This book presents a comprehensive exploration of how social psychology can be leveraged to foster social change and address complex societal challenges. Each chapter delves into different aspects of social psychology, demonstrating its application across a variety of domains to influence individual behaviors, societal norms, and institutional policies toward more equitable and sustainable outcomes.

Understanding Human Behavior and Social Influence

The initial chapters focus on the foundational principles of social psychology, particularly how individual and collective behaviors are influenced by various factors. Understanding human behavior is crucial, as it lays the groundwork for developing effective strategies to promote social change.

For instance, the book discusses how attitudes are formed and changed, emphasizing the role of persuasion techniques in shifting societal views and actions. It explores the dynamics of social influence, including conformity, obedience, and how group interactions can impact individual behavior significantly.

Addressing Social Challenges

Subsequent chapters apply these psychological insights to specific social challenges, such as prejudice and discrimination, environmental sustainability, and health. The book highlights the importance of culturally responsive teaching and the necessity of addressing psychological aspects in educational strategies to promote social equity and empowerment.

Additionally, it tackles the critical issue of environmental psychology, discussing how individuals' connections to their environment can motivate or hinder pro-environmental behaviors.

Technology's Impact on Society

With the digital age reshaping social landscapes, the book dedicates a section to the social psychology of the internet. It examines how online interactions influence offline behavior and societal norms. This includes discussions on the role of anonymity, social media echo chambers, and the polarization of public opinion.

The implications of emerging technologies like artificial intelligence and virtual reality are also explored, emphasizing their potential to transform social interactions and societal structures.

Enhancing Community Engagement and Leadership

The latter part of the book focuses on practical applications of social psychology in enhancing community wellbeing and leadership within social movements. It underscores the significance of volunteerism and the psychological motivations behind altruistic behaviors, which strengthen community ties and contribute to societal wellbeing.

Leadership in social movements is examined with an emphasis on the characteristics of effective leaders and their role in driving sustained social activism.

Future Trends and Challenges

Looking forward, the book identifies future trends and challenges in social psychology that could impact social change efforts. It discusses the necessity for social psychologists to adapt to and prepare for these changes, including the need for interdisciplinary approaches and global perspectives in research and practice.

Summary of Core Themes

Interdisciplinary Collaboration and Global Perspective: One of the recurring themes in the book is the call for a more interdisciplinary approach in social psychology. The complex nature of today's social issues often requires combining insights from various fields, such as economics, environmental science, and technology, to develop effective solutions.

Ethical Considerations and Cultural Sensitivity: The book repeatedly stresses the importance of ethical considerations and cultural sensitivity in implementing social psychology principles. Interventions must respect individual autonomy and cultural differences to be truly effective and sustainable.

Empirical Research and Application: Each chapter not only discusses theoretical frameworks but also emphasizes empirical research and real-world applications. This approach ensures that the insights and strategies discussed are grounded in practical, actionable terms.

Community and Individual Empowerment: Finally, empowering communities and individuals emerges as a crucial goal. The book advocates for initiatives that not only solve immediate problems but also build resilience and self-efficacy among individuals and communities to sustain long-term change.

By integrating theoretical knowledge with practical applications, it offers a valuable resource for anyone looking to understand the social dynamics that drive behaviors and to harness this knowledge to create a better world.

ᗞᗞᗞ

Citation And References

This book represents the culmination of extensive research and meticulous analysis, incorporating a diverse range of sources, including numerous books, scholarly studies, and personal experiences. Additionally, I have scoured various websites to gather relevant information and data essential for the compilation of this work. I have taken every precaution to ensure the accuracy of the information presented and have diligently cited all sources to acknowledge their contributions.

Despite these efforts, the possibility of inadvertent errors remains. I deeply value the insights of my readers and appreciate any feedback that can help identify and rectify such inaccuracies. I encourage you to bring any discrepancies to my attention.

Your feedback is not only welcome but crucial, as it will aid in correcting current editions and enhancing the content of future ones. I am committed to maintaining the highest standards of accuracy and reliability in my work and thank you for your support and understanding.

Additionally, I firmly uphold the principle of freedom of speech and expression as guaranteed under Article 19(1)(a) of the Constitution of India, and I respect the diverse viewpoints and expressions of all readers.

ᐳᐳᐳ

Other Books Of The Author

1. Empowering Minds: A Journey into Women's Self-Discovery and Power
2. The Dynamics of Motivation: Catalyzing Thought into Action
3. Meditation and Mental Well Being: The Path to Inner Peace and Clarity
4. The Psychology of Child Education: Nurturing Future Generations
5. Ethical Enlightenment: A Modern Guide to Living with Integrity
6. Voices of Empowerment: Stories of Women Rising Against Odds
7. Social Psychology in Everyday Life: Understanding Human Connections
8. The Essence of Motivational Speaking: Inspiring Change in Others
9. Balancing Acts: Women, Work, and the Will to Lead
10. Guiding with Grace: Raising Children with Compassion and Awareness
11. The Power of Positive Aging: Embracing Life After Fifty
12. Building Resilient Communities: Social Work in Action
13. The Ethical Educator: Principles for Teaching and Learning
14. From Insight to Impact: Social Psychology for a Better World
15. The Ethics of Empathy: A Guide to Ethical Living
16. The Science of Empowering the Self: Navigating Life's Challenges with Psychological Wisdom
17. The Mindful Conscious Leader: Meditation Techniques for Modern Management
18. Pioneering Spirit: Women's Pathways to Leadership and Empowerment
19. Feeling to Healing: The Role of Emotional Intelligence in Child Development
20. Transformative Talks and Words of Inspiration: Insights into Motivational Oratory

21. Green Ethics: A Path to Sustainable Living
22. Spiritual Integrity: Navigating Life with Moral Compassion
23. Clean Living, Clean Society: The Ethics of Cleanliness
24. Patriotic Spirits: Building a Nation on Positive Attitudes
25. Innovative Integrity & Vibrant Visions: The Ethical and Entrepreneurial Spirit of Gujarat
26. Youthful Visions, Endless Possibilities: Inspiring Ethics and Motivation in Children
27. Living Your Legacy: How to Motivate Others by Living Your Values
28. Secret of Healing Conversations: Ethical Practices in Counselling and Therapy
29. Creative Kindness: Crafting a Life of Compassion and Creativity
30. The Power of Appreciation: How Gratitude Can Transform Your Relationships
31. Bhagavad-Gita: Messages
32. Science of Art: The New Frontier of Fashion Modernism
33. Vivekananda's Virtues: A Blueprint for Modern Living
34. Empower Her: Navigating the Path to Women's Entrepreneurship
35. The Boundless Classroom: Innovations in Global Education
36. The Language of Leadership: Communicating with Authenticity and Impact
37. The Warrior's Mantra: Deciphering the Hanuman Chalisa
38. Echoes of Empathy: Transformative Stories of Social Service
39. Artful Living: Cultivating Creativity in Your Daily Routine
40. Finding Your Why: Discovering Your Passions and Charting Your Course
41. The Role of Social Media in Shaping Self-Esteem and Interpersonal Relationships among Adolescents

ppp

Contact

Dr. Minakshi Bansal
Social Activist
Ahmedabad, Gujarat, Bharat
minakshiindiag20@yahoo.com

ϧϧϧ

|| LOKAHA SAMASTHAHA SUKHINO BHAVANTU ||

• 135 •